Accidental Humor and Other Reflections

Carol Galloway

ISBN: 150303142X
ISBN-13: 9781503031425

For my mother for giving me the gifts of humor, love, and encouragement

TABLE OF CONTENTS

INTRODUCTION

Aristotle once said, "The secret to humor is surprise." I agree with that. However, there are different kinds of humor, and in my opinion, some are better than others. Let me explain. There is "Bob Hope humor," which involves memorizing jokes that someone else wrote and telling those jokes to your audience. Then there is "Paul Lynde humor," which just happens and is a part of who you are, like your hair or eye color. Some say that this type of humor is being naturally witty or having a good sense of humor. Both Bob Hope and Paul Lynde knew they were funny. But my favorite kind of humor is accidental humor, which happens when you are not trying to be funny or entertain. To me, this is humor in its purest form. Is it any wonder it often comes from the young and innocent, the unsophisticated?

Through the years, I have had the pleasure of experiencing this kind of humor with my students, grandchildren, and on one occasion a neighbor girl. Accidental humor didn't happen often, but when it did, I wrote it down. Two of my daughters, also teachers, occasionally shared their stories with me, and I have included a few of those as well.

Even in 2011, some of the children's responses sounded like they were right out of the 1950s. When I asked my second graders to complete the phrase "*If I were twenty-one, I...*" seven out of eleven girls responded by writing, "I would get married." Although some entries are not necessarily funny, they are worthy of taking note and reflecting on.

ELEMENTARY SCHOOL

In the early 1990s, I was teaching third grade in Anchorage, Alaska, and never thought about writing down my students' uninhibited commentaries or life observations. However, I'll never forget one incident. When we were discussing favorite books and making connections to our own lives, Jane, a bright, talkative nine-year-old, said, "*The Berenstain Bears and the Bad Habit* reminds me of my mom because she has a bad habit too; she smokes." A boy in the back interjected something that I could not hear. I asked him to repeat it, but it still was unclear. Then Jane decided to help me and said very loudly, "He said my mom is a pussy!" However, he actually said that her mom was a hussy.

෴

Before school, I had outdoor duty. My job was to keep the peace and discourage running, yelling, and roughhousing. One morning, a first grader came running up to me; he was visibly upset. Before I could tell him not to run, he said through the sobs, "Kenneth says I wear my mom's bra and panties!"

Not knowing how to respond, I said, "Who's Kenneth?" Just then the bell rang and we all had to proceed inside—whew, saved by the bell!

෴

During our school carnival, as I was volunteering at the hot dog booth, Dennis, one of my special education students, came up with a friend who didn't go to our school. I said hello and asked Dennis if his friend was John, a boy he often wrote about in class. Dennis nodded but looked uncomfortable. I could tell something was wrong because he was usually easygoing and talkative. It didn't take long to figure out why he was acting so strange when he proceeded to introduce me to his friend: "This is Mrs. Galloway...my lunch lady." Obviously he was concealing the fact that he was in special education classes.

❧

I had been working with my third and fourth graders on making inferences. While reading *Holes*, by Louis Sachar, I paused to ask about a character named Zero. "Zero doesn't know any nursery rhymes. What can you infer from that fact?"

Patrick enthusiastically blurted out, "He didn't have cable!"

❧

While I was writing with my students, Susan, a fifth grader, said, "My grandmother lets me play with the hanging skin on her arms." She then proceeded to demonstrate by tugging at her own skin under her arm. Gee, I wonder what made her think of that? Could it be that I was wearing a short-sleeved shirt? Teachers love for students to make connections, but some connections are better left unsaid.

෴

Halley, a fourth grader, was chatting with me before class about her upcoming sleepover. She informed me that her friend "is a little bit China and we get to eat with chopsticks!"

෴

One morning during my outdoor duty, a very unhappy second-grade boy announced that he was grounded. His classmates were not exactly sure what "grounded" meant, so he explained, "It's when you have to stay home and watch *Hooked on Phonics* videos."

෴

Our second graders were writing letters to soldiers. We brainstormed a list of words and phrases we could use in our letters, such as *sacrifice, brave,* and *defending our country*. That's why I was quite surprised with Danny's choice of words: "Dear

Soldier, I hope you don't get drunk." I guess he had some insight into how stressful war can be.

∽

One time I told a group of special education students that I had a surprise for them (we were getting a new student). Gavin, a second grader, piped up, saying, "You're going to have a baby!" Without missing a beat, Evelyn, a third grader, said, "She's too old to have a baby!"

∽

I was working with a small group of first graders, and we were talking about vitamins. I asked if they took vitamins, and Logan replied, "Yes, I take bacon bits."

∽

Jack, a third grader, was explaining to me how he recalls information when he needs it. He said, "I push play in my head."

∽

One of my colleagues was teaching a phonics lesson and was explaining the sound that the letter *x* makes. She proceeded to give an example by using the word *X-ray*, and abruptly one second grader announced, "I had my vagina x-rayed once!"

❧

We were playing a word game in which the goal was to make as many words as possible using the letters in the word *strawberry*. The kids were struggling, so I decided to give them a hint. "This is something you do at a casino."

Jim replied without hesitation, "Rob."

I told him there wasn't an *o* in strawberry. I was going for the word *bet*.

❧

My first year at one elementary school, I was the special education teacher in the resource room. After three weeks of working with the kids, Dave, a third grader, said, "Do you work here?" I knew then it was going to be a very long year.

❧

Darin asked, "Will you tie my shoe?" as he aimed his mud-caked shoe at me.

Upon noticing his shoe was already tied, I said, "Why? It is already tied."

He just stared at me, not offering an explanation. All I could figure was that he wanted me to bend over so he could look down my shirt. However, on that particular day, I was wearing a turtleneck.

∽

Dave was worried because he forgot his homework and promised he would bring it to me after school, since he lived within walking distance. After solving his problem and making a plan, he calmly sat down and was ready to get to work. Then suddenly he said, "What time do you close?"

∽

In the resource room, we were working on manners and earning tickets for good behavior. On Friday, I would draw tickets from a bowl and give out small prizes. Everyone understood that the more tickets they earned, the better their chances of getting picked for a prize. After finishing our work, I suggested that we play a game. In response, one of my fourth-grade boys said, "Instead of playing a game, can we do good behavior?" A slight disconnect there, wouldn't you say?

∽

We were discussing a story called "A Curve in the River," which is about a girl who threw a bottle with a message inside into a river. My second graders were sharing what kind of messages they would put in a bottle. Casey eagerly volunteered. "I would put plans on how to get rid of bin Laden!" I asked him if he thought those plans should be left up to the military and immediately felt guilty for crushing his idea. Then, full of confidence, he replied, "Oh no, my plan would *work!*" His dad did work for the government.

∾

While working with a small group of third graders (four boys and one girl), I gave the writing prompt "Why hasn't a woman ever been president of the United States?"

After spending ten minutes writing, we were ready to share. The boys said things like "because it would probably be a disaster" and "because she would talk on the phone all day or go shopping." I was getting a little irritated with the boys' sexist answers when the lone girl said, "Women are strong! They give birth, and men can't do that."

I was elated and said that I thought she had a valid point, but the boys were not convinced. Then a boy who had remained silent thus far said, "Playing football is a lot harder than having a baby!"

❧

A first grader in the resource room was dancing around with his hand down the back of his pants, digging away. I thought he might be trying to fix a wedgie.

Finally he pulled his hand out of his pants, and I said, "Do you think you should wash your hands?"

He proceeded to hold his palm against his face and take a long, deep sniff. Then he thrust his hand in my face and said, "No, here, smell."

I didn't even know I could jump backward, but I did.

❧

On the first day of school, my writing prompt for my second graders was "What would you like to learn this year?" I never know what I am going to get, and this particular year was full of surprises. Two were priceless:

"I would like to learn whatever you want me to learn."

"I would like to learn how girls get pregnant."

❧

We were learning the first step of the writing process (the prewrite), and I instructed my students to pick a topic they knew a lot about and write down everything that entered their brains as they thought about their topics. We call this brainstorming. After ten minutes, I asked for volunteers to share their prewrites. One of my enthusiastic second graders told the class his topic was YouTube and proceeded to read his brainstorming list: "computer, pictures, singing, soccer" and then, without hesitation, "bedroom videos." That's what you get when you ask students to write down whatever pops into their heads! There isn't much of a filter system at age seven.

∽

The class was getting louder and louder as I walked around the room responding and supporting my young writers. Out of complete frustration, using my outside voice to be heard above the rumble, I said to another staff member working in the room, "Is there detention today?"

She replied, "I believe so."

Dead silence! It amazed me how motivated my students could be with just a few words of encouragement.

∽

Karl, a second grader, approached me first thing Monday morning wielding a water bottle with the cap removed. He thrust the bottle up to my face and said, "Guess what that smell is?"

I took a whiff of the empty bottle but couldn't identify any particular smell. I said to Karl, "I have a cold, so that might be why I can't smell it."

He had me smell it again to no avail. He was becoming impatient with the guessing game and revealed the mystery smell, saying, "My mom took it to the science fair Friday night with wine in it! She says it calms her down."

❧

It was Friday, and I was dressed more casually than usual because I was out of ironed pants. I was wearing blue jeans and white tennis shoes with blue stripes. This was a first for me because I usually looked much more professional. One of my second graders kept staring at me with a puzzled look on her face. Finally, she said, "Where are you going in those clothes?"

❧

On Monday mornings, we would gather on the rug for "check-in," a time for students to talk about their weekends. Most seven- and eight-year-olds love to talk, especially about themselves. That is why their sentences always began with "The best part of my weekend was…" They learned to prioritize, and it was truly one of their favorite activities. The primary goal for check-in was to build relationships.

On this particular morning, Terry was waving her hand high in the air like she was directing traffic. When it was her turn, she said, "The best part of my weekend was having a party!"

Trying to draw her out a little more, I asked, "Why did you have a party? What was the occasion?"

She spoke up without hesitation. "The grown-ups wanted to get drunk!"

౷

Week after week, bits of the children's lives would unfold at our Monday-morning check-ins. On one Monday morning, a quiet second grader enthusiastically shared, "The best part of my weekend was church. We had hip-hop Sunday!"

౷

We were learning that every word must have a vowel. We were using the letters *t, c, m, b, f, s,* and *a* to make words. A second grader shared her word, *tam.* Puzzled, I said, "What does that word mean?"

Showing her frustration, she replied, "You know, those things women wear on their periods."

৵

Teaching can be a real juggling act, and fulfilling all your responsibilities and duties can be challenging. I had to test a girl one-on-one for special education, so I instructed my five students in the resource room for math to work quietly in their workbooks. Later that day, I was looking over their work when one boy's answer caught my eye. He had written, "Answers will vary." I had failed to take out the answer key in the back of the workbook.

৵

Toward the end of the year, I asked students to write about the most important thing they learned in second grade. Here are some of those responses:

"The most important thing I learned in second grade was you do not always get to have your way."

"The most important thing I learned in second grade was regroping." (I'm pretty sure he meant *regrouping*.)

"The most important thing I learned in second grade was math, because if you are a girl, you buy lots of stuff. I need to buy clothes, makeup, jewelry, a house, and baby clothes."

"The most important thing I learned in second grade was telling time, because if it's dinner and you don't know the time and you are an adult, you won't know when you are supposed to cook dinner. And if you have kids and a wife, they are going to starve. Why? Because they need to eat, and if you don't feed them for three days, they are going to die. But if you feed them, they are going to live. What's better, dying or living? Living, because you get to learn and go swimming and also go camping. But if you die, you can't do as much."

"The most important thing I learned in second grade was PE/physical exercise because PE helps you get fit, and it's fun. Yes, getting fit is fun. Most of you people reading this already know this stuff, but it's always good hearing it another time."

಄

The daily prompt was "I know how to...First you..." Colin, a second grader, wrote, "I know how to watch a movie. First you get a chair, then popcorn, and then a movie."

಄

My students wrote every day, and I wrote alongside them. On this particular day, I had a substitute teacher for one of my thirty-minute writing classes for my special education students. When I returned the next day, the sub had left me a note saying, "Ken and Alicia both wrote the whole time. I couldn't get them to stop!" That made my day.

❦

Vincent, a new student in our class, wrote *Connor* on his spelling test paper. When I inquired, he told me his real name was Connor and his nickname was Vincent. I was a tad suspicious and told him I would have to go by the name in his school records for reporting purposes. I explained that usually a nickname for Vincent would be Vince, not Connor. He stuck to his story, and later in the day, he wrote a different name (not Vincent or Connor) on his paper. When I asked him why he was putting yet another name on his paper, he replied, "That's my last name's nickname."

❦

After hearing comments such as "She's making fun of my drawing" and "He said I couldn't play," I decided to talk to my second graders to encourage them to stop and think about their actions. We discussed hurt feelings and the Golden Rule: treat others how you want to be treated. The discourse was going so well that I decided to bump it up a notch and said, "If you can't get along with others, how do you think it could affect your future?" I was trying to get them to see beyond today and hoping employment and getting a job were on their radars.

All I got was several bewildered faces staring at me. Then an excited Katrina raised her hand and said, "You wouldn't be able to get a husband!"

 ∽

Second graders love to share their writing, and better yet, they love a captive audience. On this particular day, Anna was in front of the class reading from her journal. She was a good student and always did her best, but this time she had definitely outdone herself. I listened intently and was amazed. I could hear her "voice"—that individual style unique to a person's writing, something you rarely see in a second grader. She wrote about not liking to play outside and the sun being over-rated and giving her mom wrinkles. She used words such as "flabbergasted" and "unfortunate." I was mesmerized, and my thoughts turned to what part I may have played as her teacher in this brilliant piece of writing. When she finished, I couldn't praise her enough. I told her that this was one of the best pieces of writing I had ever seen from a second grader. I then asked her if I could make a copy to use as a model for excellent writing. She proudly handed over her master-piece. I was so impressed with her that I couldn't stop smiling—until I heard a boy from the back of the room yell, "Did you get that from *The Diary of a Wimpy Kid?*"

And she replied proudly, "Yes." She had copied word for word from the book. I was crushed.

ᕤ

In science, we were studying rocks and learning how to sort them into different categories. My first question to my group of second graders was to ask them how rocks are different. An eager boy named Karl replied, "They can't fly!"

ᕤ

We practiced sorting rocks by color and size, and then I instructed the students to work in groups of two to find additional ways to sort rocks. I went around checking their categories to see how they were working through the task. They were coming up with a variety of categories (shiny, dull, round, flat, etc.). Then I spotted a category labeled "weird." I asked what they meant, and they replied, "Look at these; aren't they weird?"

ᕤ

We were discussing spelling words and their meanings. When I introduced the word *hygiene,*

Harriet proceeded to share her expertise on the word by saying, "My mom says my dad doesn't have very good hygiene, and he needs to wash his hair, and he needs to clean his ears because he has all this goop in them."

∽

During the year, we read Washington Children's Choice Picture Book Award nominees. After reading each book, the students would evaluate it. They rated the book on a scale of one (worst) to five (the best) and gave a brief rationale as to why they gave it that score. Jason wrote, "It didn't impress me that much, but I don't want Mrs. Galloway to be depressed, so I put two stars for my rating."

∽

Another writing prompt asked what friendship looks like. Norm wrote, "I know Jake is my friend because he gives me stuff and plays with me, and he likes stuff I like, and I like what he likes, and he knows what I know, and I know what he knows." Pretty much sums it up, don't you think?

∽

You would think a second grader would not be a deep thinker because second graders are too busy playing and having fun, right? Well, every once in a while, you encounter a deep thinker, such as in Keith's response to the writing prompt "What is the hardest thing about growing up and why?"

"The hardest thing about growing up is making money to survive, because I will need money to buy food and pay off the house. I need it for allowances to give the kids. And money for college for the kids."

∽

Another deep thinker, Fern, wrote, "The hardest thing about growing up is when you get older, you die. And when you get older, your family members die. You get sad and sadder."

∽

The wise words of three students:
Lance wrote, "The hardest thing about growing up is helping people with their homework, because when they get it wrong, you have to go over the instructions again. And then they still get it wrong, and you yell at them because you want to be done with it."

∽

Robert wrote, "The hardest part about growing up is finding a house. Why? Because you have to pay for it."

∽

Kathy wrote, "The hardest thing about growing up is learning to mow the grass. My mom's way is too hard. My dad's way is easy."

∽

Students were to complete the following phrases:
What I want most in the world is..."Tacos."
I feel sorry for..."You."
When someone hurts me, I... "Rub it."
I am really good at..."Running in high heels."
I never want to forget..."My name."
I never want to forget..."My backpack."
Sometimes I dream about..."Having babies."
When I was little..."I looked good."
My favorite time of day is..."Night."
My favorite time of day is..."Church."
My favorite time of day is..."November."
I wish I could..."Have babies."
I would rather read than..."Get chicken pox."
I would rather read than..."Fall off a cliff."
I would rather read than..."Get hurt."

∽

Writing Prompt: Do you think life is harder for a girl or boy? Or do you think there is no difference at all? Explain your answer.

21

Zach: "Boys' lives are harder because boys are the ones who get in trouble a lot."

Julie: "A girl because if a girl wants to wear what she wants to wear, her parents say no."

Devin: "A girl's life is harder because it takes her longer to get dressed, and her haircuts are more expensive than boys'."

Renee: "There is no difference at all because it depends on if your life is hard. If you have to take care of a dog, like me, it is a pain in the butt. If dogs annoy you, then you are on the same page as me."

Kevin: "Life is harder for a girl if she is your big sister, because babysitting your brother is always a problem."

Mason: "I think life is harder for a boy because boys make bad choices. And boys have to watch their little brother, and sometimes their brother messes up the house, and you have to clean it up."

Anita: "What's hard is being a girl, because when you go through puberty and have a baby, it's very, very hard if you're a teenager. When you are an adult, that is the hardest because you have to find a good husband to take care of your baby or babies."

Anne: "It's harder for boys because they have to mow the lawn and paint the house. PS My dad doesn't do that stuff. And my mom does some hard work, but she's not into rushing into her work."

Melody: "I think it is harder for boys because they take a lot of time to eat and talk too much at work, like my mom's friend Brandon."

John: "I think there is no difference at all because you both argue a lot and take care of babies."

∽

Writing Prompt: It's thirty years in the future, and you are famous. You are on the cover of a magazine. Write why you are famous.

"I am thirty-eight years old. I'm pretty even though I'm old. I look cranky. I can exercise, but it hurts."

"If I were famous, it would be because I was a superstar in a pie-eating contest. I win a bronze metal and a trophy."

"If I was on the cover of a magazine, I would go on the red carpet. I would meet famous people and stay up all night and eat really good snacks!"

∽

Prompt: Give directions for how to do something (e.g., ride a bike). List the steps.

Chuck wrote: How to make a dog sit
1. First, get a dog.
2. Second, tell it to sit.
3. If it doesn't listen, do it again and again.

❦

I was testing Aaron on synonyms and asked him what word meant the same as sleep. He answered, "Passed out." I then told him we were about to do the last part of the test, and he replied, "Dessert?"

❦

One morning, Martin, an extremely overactive, talkative boy, was trying to fit his small body into a backpack. He blurted out to me, "I may seem crazy because I'm half Indian." I'm pretty sure he is Norwegian. He has blond hair and blue eyes.

❦

During check-in one Monday, Ashley shared, "The best part of my weekend was that I got to ride a murdercycle." Her classmates quickly corrected her, telling her the word was *motor*, not *murder*.

❦

One day, I was giving Brandy a three-minute timed test on addition and subtraction facts. I told her not to erase but to cross out, to skip hard ones, and to work as fast as she could. Halfway through the test, she stopped, looked up at me, and said, "Am I working as fast as I can?"

∾

One day Maddy announced that her favorite food was "roast beast."

∾

On a Monday morning, a new boy arrived in our class, and Alicia asked, "Does Jackson work here?" She was referring to schoolwork. She sure had the right idea about school.

∾

One day Josh came up to me and said, "I saw what you were wearing yesterday."

I inquired, "What was that?"

He said, "You know, that thing in the back of your hair." He meant a hair clip. He went on to tell me that when his mother wears her hair up like that, it makes her look younger.

I could not resist and said, "Does it make me look younger?"

Without skipping a beat, he said, "No!"

∾

Sometimes kids can make your day by their kind words of appreciation or concern. One morning Maria, a sweet Hispanic girl, came up to me and gave me what I'm sure she considered a compliment. With a wide, sincere smile, she said, "You smell just like my grandma."

Of course I was hoping her grandma wasn't dead when I replied, "I hope she smells good."

Maria answered, "Yes, she smells just like you."

❧

There is something in a young person's mind that makes him or her exaggerate to the point of absurdity. For example, on the first day of school, one of our activities was interviewing our classmates. One of the questions was to name an accomplishment that the student is proud of.

Dennis, a confident young man, said, "I was a stunt person and did backflips on my bike."

❧

Another question was "What interesting fact about yourself can you share with me?"

Kane said, "I sleep on my side."

Another boy replied, "Once I dreamed I was a ballerina."

❧

To the question "What is your favorite hobby?" Kane replied, "Goofing around."

∽

Yet another interview question was to tell your classmate something he or she may not know about you. Cora replied, "I have 105 pets." Now, the boy interviewing her was not going to stop there. He wanted to know what kinds of pets and of course their names. Cora was not backing down, and every time she opened her mouth, her story got more bizarre. Some of her pets included kangaroos, water buffalos, and tigers.

One thing you can say about young people is that they will not recant even when it is evident they are not being truthful (i.e., lying). When Cora was asked follow-up questions, such how much it cost to feed all those animals ("$672 a day") and where she lived ("Lakewood"), she continued to calmly answer without seeming the least bit rattled.

∽

My second graders would write every morning, and those who wanted to share brought their journals with them to the rug when we did our morning routine (e.g., calendar, agenda for the day, and so forth). The prompt for the day was "If

I could fly…" I was surprised when Chuck eagerly brought his journal to the rug. Chuck usually kept his thoughts to himself and rarely put them on paper. I called on him first, and with a wide smile, he stood in front of his classmates and read, "If I could fly, I would shoot all the birds and make them poop on people." Complete hysteria ensued—the exact reaction he was looking for. Yes, potty humor is definitely a skill most second-grade boys possess, and ever so proudly.

∽

One day Keith asked me how old I was. I replied, "Don't you know you should never ask a woman how old she is?" He entertained that thought for a moment but then persisted. I tried to ignore him, but finally he got the best of me, and I told him I would tell him if he promised not to tell anyone else. He agreed. I then whispered that I was born in 1946.

He just gave me a bewildered look and said, "Come on, you said you would tell me how old you are."

I replied, "Do the math!"

Clearly frustrated, he replied, "I already did my math this morning and turned it in!"

∽

All week we had been reading books on Martin Luther King Jr. and even watched a recording of his "I Have a Dream" speech. I gave the students an assignment they had to complete before recess. The instructions were to write down three things they had learned about Martin Luther King Jr.

Crystal wrote, "Martin Luther King was a good king."

                    ⚬

We took our second-grade classes to see a play, *Junie B. Jones*, at the Pantages Theater in Tacoma, Washington. Many of the kids had never been to a live performance and were in awe of the whole experience. They had never seen anything like the building before. The inside was like a palace with ornate gold shapes and designs throughout, even on the ceiling. The seats were comfortable and covered in what looked like red velvet. We had great seats in the front rows of the balcony. As we awaited the start of the play, one of my boys said, "I wish we could sit over there," and pointed to the box seats on the sides of the theater. Then I heard a girl say, "You can't sit there! Those seats are for Oprah!"

                    ⚬

My daughter Lynne, a teacher, was walking her third graders to lunch when she overheard one of her students, a Somalian girl, say, "I hate Jews!"

Lynne was stunned and immediately confronted her saying, "You can't say that. How would you like it if someone said they hated your hijab (headdress)?" The girl looked confused until a boy standing near her said, "She said 'I hate juice'!"

⁓

My grandson Nicholas was part of a group discussion in his third-grade classroom when a classmate started to talk about his father. The boy said, "My dad's name is Dick."

Instantly Nicholas shouted out a warning to his classmate: "Don't even go there!"

⁓

My daughter Tiffany was quietly talking to one of her third-grade students about how important it is to be a good listener. The girl did not have a clue what was going on and complained that she wasn't on task, because she didn't know what she was supposed to be doing.

I know how frustrating this can be for a teacher because you spend so much time going over (and over) the task you want students to do, asking if there are any questions, giving examples, and even doing some of the assignment with the whole class. My daughter patiently (again) went over the assignment step by step and again expressed how important it is to be a good listener. She told the student she could miss out on critical and even lifesaving information if she didn't pay attention to what was going on around her. Feeling good about taking the time to talk to her and giving her every opportunity to be successful, Tiffany asked, "Are you ready to get to work?"

The young girl looked up at her and said, "Your breath stinks!"

❧

My daughter Lynne was facilitating a book club of her second-grade students who were reading a *Little House on the Prairie* book. As teachers do, she stopped the group periodically and asked a question to check for understanding or go over a vocabulary word that they might not be familiar with. On this particular day, she asked the group why building on the bank could be dangerous. After some thought, a boy responded, "Because banks get robbed." Teachers are always trying to guide students in making a connection to their own lives.

THOUGHTS ON TEACHING

Teaching is a lot like being a parent; you have no idea what is in store for you. You can be knowledgeable and confident and seek the expertise of professionals, but it still can all go to hell in an instant. It also can feel like a thankless job. Both jobs are grueling and take up all your time and energy. Kids just don't appreciate all you do for them, but that isn't the reason you become a parent or a teacher.

When I started teaching elementary school, the kids said I reminded them of Lucille Ball. I was fine with that and in fact took it as a compliment. I watched the *I Love Lucy* show growing up, and it always made me laugh. After about eight years, I decided to move on and try my hand at junior high school. What was I thinking? Well, I got the writing bug and thought I would have more opportunities to do what I loved: write.

I have no idea what happened, but my *I Love Lucy* persona was gone.

Early on in my junior high career, some girls (fifteen going on thirty) said I reminded them of Judge Judy. At the time, I had no idea who Judge Judy was. When I saw her on television, I wasn't sure if they were referring to her looks or the way she acted. I'm pretty sure it was their way of calling me a bitch.

The following comprises some snippets of my days teaching teenagers. I gave it my best for four

years (two of the four in high school) before I
returned to elementary school, where I remained
until I retired in 2012.

JUNIOR HIGH AND HIGH SCHOOL

After several turbulent days with my ninth-grade English class, I gave the following writing prompt: "How does your behavior in class add or detract from the learning environment?" One girl wrote, "Young teachers should teach because if teachers are young, they're more likely to put up with our crap." I was fifty-three.

∽

In my ninth-grade English class, I said, "Raise your hand if you have ever read poetry."

Brenda popped up and said, "Voluntarily?"

∽

One day I had the whole class stand up and move to one side of the classroom. I asked them to cross the room if they had ever defied authority. Right away, Barbara said, "I don't even know what that means!"

Before I could respond, her friend Katie said, "Believe me, it's you!"

∽

I had written *dramatic irony* on the whiteboard for a lesson that afternoon. Dana, a bright ninth grader, began the discussion by saying, "Dramatic irony sounds like my life!"

39

❧

Getting ninth graders excited and engaged in the learning process can be challenging. However, I'm usually pleasantly surprised by how interested they are in poetry. That was the case with Michael. Most of the semester, he sat in his seat like it was an upright bed—eyes barely open, head tilted back, and mouth open like a baby bird waiting to be fed. Oh, the power of poetry! Michael could not stop writing. Special moments like this help a teacher put aside all those stressful days that make her doubt her vocation and instead celebrate. The students were preparing to present their poems the next day, and Michael was eager to share—so eager, in fact, that he said to me, poem in hand, "I'm glad I get to read this to the class tomorrow because I don't think I can write this again." Something told me I should take a look at his "masterpiece" and not wait to hear it the next day, which was a good call because the poem was obscene, and I could not let him read it to the class.

❧

I was teaching at an "alternative" high school, and it was the beginning of the year. Each day I collected the school fees that the students were required to pay. One of the fees was a computer usage fee, and after several weeks of hearing my pitch on how important it was to bring the ten-dollar fee, everyone but one boy had paid. I began to pressure him so he could start researching for an internship.

Every day when he first arrived, I asked him if he had brought his ten dollars. Every day he said that he had forgotten. One day he did not show up. Pretty soon everyone was talking about him, and I asked what happened. A student told me that at his bus stop, he robbed another student and was arrested. Oops! I may have come on a little strong about the ten-dollar fee.

AT HOME

One morning as my five-year-old grandson, Everett, was getting ready for school, he told me he was feeling "intermostic." When I asked him what the word meant, he answered without the slightest hesitation, "It means your brain is a little smart."

❧

Everett was having a last-day-of-school party at his house for his fifth-grade classmates. It was a sunny day, and the kids were outside playing croquet. Everett's mom, Lynne, was trying to stay out of the way and give them some freedom to be kids. As she stood on the upstairs deck of her bedroom, she heard her eleven-year-old son yell, "OK, everyone, listen up! Who here is a virgin?"

❧

My grandson Everett's Christmas list:
Dear Santa,
Here is a list of things I would like for Christmas:
- Beatles Rock Band
- $25
- A beard stubble
- A moustache
- A girlfriend
- A girlfriend for Alec
- Muscles

ᑐᕀ

When I told my grandson Everett that I taught special education, he said, "What's special education—something old people teach?"

ᑐᕀ

On another occasion, Everett told me that he was almost as tall as his mom, his feet were almost as big, and his head was the same size. I asked, "What about brains—whose is bigger?"

Without hesitation, he replied, "Mine is a little bigger because she couldn't figure out how to do my computer game, and it's third-grade level, *and* she teaches third grade!"

ᑐᕀ

Residing at our house, as she has for more than fifteen years, is a lifelike, six-foot-tall stuffed doll we call Inez. She is an older, matronly looking woman who wears glasses. I carefully pick out clothes for her to wear depending on the season. In the summer, she wears capris, a T-shirt, and a visor and sunglasses. Sometimes I place a badminton racket on her lap for effect. Shortly after receiving Inez as a birthday present from my daughters, I saw our seven-year-old neighbor, Jordan, peeking in the window.

Several weeks later, while my husband, Steve, was working in the yard, Jordan approached him and asked, "Do you have fake people in your house?"

Not understanding her question, he replied, "What do you mean?"

Jordan repeated, "Do you have fake people in your house?"

It finally dawned on him that she was referring to Inez, and he said, "Oh, that's Carol's doll."

Jordan looked totally perplexed and remained silent for a short time. Finally, she said, "How old is Carol?" Steve told her I was fifty, and she replied, "Isn't Carol a little old for a doll?"

༄

Everett had tears in his eyes when he asked his mom, "Are you and Papa getting a divorce?"

Lynne was shocked and could not figure out why he would say such a thing. She thought maybe he had heard them argue or perhaps heard her call his dad an ass. Confused and surprised by his question, she said, "Why do you think that?"

Everett replied, "Because you're a rooster and Papa's a rabbit!" He had read on the place mat at a local Chinese restaurant that his mom and dad were "opposite signs" in the Chinese zodiac and "not a good match."

Lynne asked Nicholas, her six-year-old nephew, if he liked his mom's boyfriend. Nicholas replied, "He keeps telling me he told me three times to stop, but I never heard him. Maybe I need a haircut." His hair had grown over his ears.

ON THE ROAD

My husband and I used to take our two oldest grandchildren to the ocean once a year. On one such trip, Ben, seven, and Marissa, ten, sat in the backseat anticipating the five-hour drive. Suddenly Ben said, "What will we do next year when Marissa gets her period? She'll attract sharks!" After composing myself, I asked him where he heard that, and he replied, "On *The Cosby Show*."

❧

Our daughter Tiffany arrived at our home with her four-year-old son, Stevie, still fast asleep in his car seat. She asked Steve, her dad, to please get Stevie out of the car. As he was lifting the armrest and unbuckling the strap, Stevie bolted awake, frantically yelling, "Don't mess my hair up! Don't touch my hair!" He had carefully perfected his "look" before he left home. His bangs were evenly separated into strands that he had coated with gel.

❧

One day when Ben and his brother, Stevie, sat in the back seat eating apple slices and string cheese, Ben announced out of the blue, "I'm like my dad because I like old people and babies, and

Stevie is like his mom because he likes to squeeze pimples."

∽

During a long car ride, I asked Ben and Stevie if they had a favorite sport. Stevie, age five, enthusiastically replied, "I'm going to play basketball someday!"

Ben quickly crushed his dream by saying, "You can't be a basketball player; you're a midget!"

∽

My daughter Lynne and four-year-old grandson, Everett, stopped by for a visit. It had started to snow, and my husband said to Everett, "So what do you think of the snow?"

Without hesitation, Everett answered, "I have been waiting years for this!" The operative word is *years*.

∽

My daughter was at the dentist's office with her three-year-old for a checkup. They sat in the hard, cloth-covered maroon chairs waiting their turn. The office was quiet, with only background music playing to soothe the apprehensive patients. Everyone kept to themselves, reading, dozing off, or playing with handheld devices. Everett jumped up and ran over to a table with books and magazines stacked on top of it. He selected a book that had bright, colorful illustrations and brought it back to his chair. He proceeded to ask his mom questions about the strangely dressed men. Lynne told him it was a children's Bible. Everett didn't say anything at first but then in a loud voice said, "What's a Bible?"

Not wanting to elaborate further, his mom replied, "A book."

Everett replied, "When I get home, I'm gonna write a Bible."

∽

Steve and I were at a restaurant with our granddaughters, Marissa and Naomi. We were looking at our menus and trying to decide what we wanted for breakfast when Naomi, age eight, turned to me and said, "Can we get appetizers?"

PARTING WORDS

Children and how they see the world around them is often priceless and humorous. Everyone at sometime or another gets to witness that. This book represents a living document of some of those moments and is a way to preserve and share them with others. As Anaïs Nin said, "We write to taste life twice."

ABOUT THE AUTHOR

Carol Galloway is a retired teacher. She received her Bachelor of Arts from the University of Puget Sound and her Masters in Education at City University. She has published poems in the Tacoma *News Tribune* and *The Hand Of Destiny*. This is her first book. Carol lives in Washington State on Anderson Island with her husband.

18040289R00040

Made in the USA
San Bernardino, CA
29 December 2014